Wet, Wet,

Written by Helen Greathead

Collins

Dark clouds are rain clouds.

Rain plops on the ground and
the ground gets wet. Rain can be
good, or bad.

Plants need the rain and sun.
Rain keeps the soil soft.

The land gets hard and cracks
with no rain. Plants die in
the hot ground.

dam

tap

Rain fills up the big dam.
We drink rain from the dam out
of the tap.

Rain is good for the farm. Cows drink the rain.

The clouds are darker in a storm.
Lots of rain cannot drain into
the ground.

Too much rain is bad. It can sweep
cars off the road.

If it is chilly, rain can come as hail. Hail can be big. Hail hits the ground hard.

In winter the ground can freeze.
Cars slide on the frozen ground.

We need rain to drink. Plants need rain too.

We need rain but too much rain
is bad.

Good rain

Bad rain

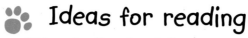

Ideas for reading

Written by Clare Dowdall BA(Ed), MA(Ed)
Lecturer and Primary Literacy Consultant

Learning objectives: recognise common digraphs; read a range of familiar and common words and simple sentences independently; extend their vocabulary, exploring the meanings and sounds of new words; use phonic knowledge to write simple regular words; show an understanding of how information can be found in non-fiction books to answer questions about where, who, why and how; use talk to organise, sequence and clarify thinking, ideas, feelings and events

Curriculum links: Understanding the World: The world

Focus phonemes: a, ai, ou (cloud), oo (good), ee, ow, oa, ar, y (ee), o-e, z

Fast words: are, the, we, come

Word count: 150

Getting started

- Fast read some words from the text that contain the focus phonemes, e.g. rain, cloud, good, need, road. Add sound buttons and lines for each phoneme. Practise reading the words again.

- Read the title together. Discuss what is happening on the front cover, providing new vocabulary to help children describe what they can see, e.g. umbrella, rain, flood, floating.

- Ask children to describe why the book is called *Wet, Wet, Wet* and to suggest where rain comes from.

- Read the blurb together. Puzzle aloud over why rain can be good or bad, e.g. *I wonder what this means ...* Ask children to suggest when it is good and bad, and make a list of their ideas against the headings, *Rain is good when; Rain is bad when.*

Reading and responding

- Turn to pp2–3. Look at the picture of the rain clouds, and ask one child to read the text. Discuss how some of the phonemes in each word are short and some are longer, and how some phonemes are represented by two letter shapes (digraphs).